# Middle School Rules of

## MIKE EVANS

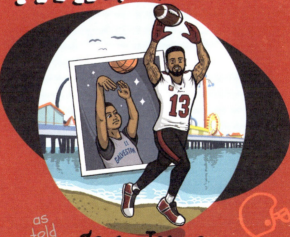

as told by *Sean Jensen*

**BroadStreet** KIDS

BroadStreet Kids
Savage, Minnesota, USA

BroadStreet Kids is an imprint of BroadStreet Publishing Group, LLC.
Broadstreetpublishing.com

# The Middle School Rules of Mike Evans

© 2023 Mike Evans and Sean Jensen
Illustrations by Daniel Hawkins

978-1-4245-6405-7
978-1-4245-6406-4 (e-book)

Back cover photo courtesy of Tampa Bay Buccaneers. Used with permission.

Design by Chris Garborg | garborgdesign.com
Edited by Michelle Winger | literallyprecise.com

Printed in China.

23  24  25  26  27  28  29    7  6  5  4  3  2  1

TABLE OF CONTENTS

# INTRODUCTION

Dear Reader,

When you're a kid, you don't understand the impact of certain situations you are in. I had bad things happen in my childhood, but I had it easier than some because I had a great community behind me. I had Coach Petteway, Aunt Josephine, Nanny Goat, and, of course, my mom.

As an adult, I realize the impossible situations Momma faced, but she did an unbelievable job of making sure our family had everything we needed.

People sometimes ask me what I would change about my story if I had the opportunity. As crazy as it may sound, I wouldn't want to change anything. Yes, I had some tough times, but everything I went through shaped me into the man I am today.

And how about this?

You are about to read my story, written by a great author. I remember reading a Middle School Rules® book to my daughter Mackenzie. She really liked the book, and I thought, *What a great way for me to reach kids!*

I love being able to help children because I know what it's like to be a kid in need.

I want to entertain you with my stories, but more than that, I want to give you hope. Life is a blessing. Everyone goes through their own adversities, trials, and struggles, and somebody else's story is maybe even worse than yours, but you get to choose what you focus on. You have an incredible opportunity to find things in your life that you can be grateful for. Connect with people who encourage you to be better. This is how you stay strong and keep fighting for your dreams.

Be the best you can be for yourself and for your family and remember... it's a blessing to be alive!

# FOREWORD BY
# Heather Kilgore
## MOMMA

When Mikey was a little boy, he had so much energy. When my male friends would come by the house, Mikey, out of nowhere, would jump on their backs, and they'd be like, "Whoa! What the heck is going on?!" I would be so embarrassed, but now that I think back on that, it's funny to me.

Mikey made friends easily, and he always had them living with us. That was hard when I was making $30,000 a year. He and his friends would eat and drink everything in the house and make a mess. I would get mad at times, but I also felt sorry for the boys. They needed a safe environment to live in, and I could relate. I sometimes lived with friends when I was growing up too.

Although he got into a little trouble, Mikey was generally a good kid. I noticed his great work ethic in high school, and I figured he would be ok. He had a good head on his shoulders. There were plenty of opportunities for Mikey to be steered in the wrong direction, but he stayed strong. He skipped parties on weekends because he was always playing in games and tournaments.

Mikey had interest from colleges for basketball pretty early on. I liked that because college programs made sure the young athletes got tutoring, and the coaches and professors helped teach the boys how to be men.

I didn't have any idea that Mikey could be a professional athlete until he was in college. That's when I noticed his talent was next level. But a Super Bowl champion? A Pro Bowl player? I still don't believe it. It feels surreal. I keep thinking I'm going to wake up from this incredible dream.

Of all the commendable things Mikey has done, I'm most proud that he's a good daddy. He loves his kids and takes care of their needs, trying to include them wherever he can.

As his momma, I think he does too much. When a teammate asks him to attend a foundation event, Mikey will always go. I often wonder how he doesn't get tired.

Recently, as I was writing checks, I thought back to those early years. The expenses were piled up on the table, and I was in tears because I didn't know how I was going to pay for everything. I took a picture of my current bills and sent Mikey a message saying, "Thanks to you, I don't have to worry anymore."

# FOREWORD BY
## Terry Petteway
### COACH

---

I have coached thousands of kids in my hometown of Galveston throughout my life.

When he showed up to his first practice at eight years old, Mike Evans was a skinny, quiet kid. He blended in and had an ok first season, but he always came to practice, and he just kept getting better and better.

In Mike's second season, I started getting him the football. He wasn't the biggest kid, or the fastest, but he would always make the first defender miss. Our quarterback would drop back and quickly dump it to Mike, who would then turn it into a 67-yard touchdown! He was so elusive; he would change direction before anyone had a chance to wrap him up, then he'd accelerate and be gone. It was a God-given talent. I don't ever remember him dropping the ball.

After his dad passed away, Mike gravitated toward me, and he developed real respect for me because he knew I had his back. He also knew he always had a ride home, and he could eat with my family. Mike is not the only kid I've fed, clothed, and housed through the years.

When Mike went to play in middle school, I told the coaches, "Get Mike the football." But they wouldn't do it. In high school, it was the same story. "Throw the ball to Mike!" I encouraged. They didn't. So, he stopped playing... until his senior year.

By then, Mike was a complete animal. The coaches used him as a decoy, but they still wouldn't throw him the ball! Imagine how much more successful the high school team would have been if Mike had been playing all those years.

Mike Evans was a big deal in Galveston County, but it took a while for people to really see how extraordinary the kid was. People love him, and his reputation has been elevated tremendously because he's "that guy" on and off the field.

Being around Mike when he's home now sometimes drives me crazy. Somebody always wants to take a picture with him or get an autograph while we're eating, and Mike will do it even though his food gets cold. He hasn't let his fame go to his head.

Mike is just a different guy, and that's what makes him special.

CHAPTER 1

# STEALING KIA'S BINKY

My mom's name is Heather, and my dad's name is Michael, but everyone calls him by his nickname, Mickey. Both of my parents had a rough childhood. Their families were poor, and their lives were chaotic.

My mom grew up in Gun Barrel City, where she picked up her accent. Her family moved to Florida to look for job opportunities, but her parents couldn't find anything meaningful, so they moved to Galveston. The family continued to struggle financially, and they had a hard time avoiding their addictions.

My parents were very young when I was born.

Everyone told me I was a very active baby. I was always getting into mischief—especially because I loved wrestling so much. I would try to mirror professional wrestling moves with friends, recreating matches with different toys... including the dolls of my sister Mikia (who everyone called Kia).

My favorite wrestlers were The Rock and Stone Cold Steve Austin. I can't remember how many times Kia's dolls were on the receiving end of a Stone Cold Stunner: his finishing move.

Sometimes when I was bored, I would bother Kia, who is ten months younger than me. I would annoy her all the time by taking her stuff. Her crying didn't bother me.

I didn't like pacifiers but Kia did. We called it a *binky*, and I would steal it right out of Kia's mouth just to upset her. I'm not sure why I did that so much.

As we got older, Kia and I called our parents *Momma* and *Daddy*. Like our parents, we had a lot of challenges in our early years. Because they were so young, my parents didn't have steady jobs, so money was always tight. Their families could barely take care of themselves let alone help us.

We had to move several times, but I don't really remember because I was pretty young. Momma doesn't like to talk about those early years very much. It was hard and scary for her.

CHAPTER 2

# SUPERHERO

We always lived with our momma. Daddy would often disappear, sometimes for a long time. We heard about some negative things he may have been doing, but Kia and I both saw him the same way: as our superhero!

Daddy dreamed of being a professional basketball player, and he was really good, but he dropped out of high school, so he could only play at local parks and gyms. He would find as many pickup games as he could.

Dad would take Kia and me to watch him play at Alamo Park, and we always thought he was the best player!

Momma was young, and we didn't have any money. Daddy not being around put even more pressure on her to take care of us. Kia and I would get upset more often with Momma because the three of us were always together.

Daddy was tall and really strong. He could jump high and do 100 push-ups in a row! He made me do push-ups with him, and he always told me how important it was to be physically fit.

Daddy's Rule:
Stay active, so your body
feels good and strong.

CHAPTER 3

# LEARNING TO RIDE A BIKE

Momma's mother was a strong presence in my life. When I was just starting to talk, she wanted me to call her "Nana." But I could only say "Na" or "Nan."

One day, Nana read me the story, "The Three Billy Goats Gruff."

You're a boy goat, and I'm a Nanny Goat.

Nanny Goat.

The name stuck! Everyone knows my nana as Nanny Goat.

Nanny Goat had taught a few kids to ride their bikes in a parking lot across the street from her house.

I wanted to learn how to ride, but I was only three years old.

Nanny Goat wasn't nervous at all.

It's OK to fall, but you have to get back up.

Nanny Goat's Rule:
You're going to fall,
but you have to get
right back up!

CHAPTER 4

# SHARED BIRTHDAYS

Momma did the best she could. We always had food to eat, and she kept our house clean, but she struggled to support us financially. Sometimes, our air conditioning would get cut off because Momma couldn't

afford to pay the electric bill. That's a problem

in Galveston, Texas, where the average temperature

between May and October is over 80 degrees! We

would stay with someone else when we couldn't use

our air conditioning.

One way Momma saved money was to do a

combined birthday party for Kia and me—even

though our birthdays were two months apart. Kids

loved coming to our house for our birthday parties.

Sometimes we'd have a blow-up pool party, but our

favorite was the one time we got a big inflatable

Caterpillar with an obstacle course and slide. We raced around that course what felt like a hundred times each.

We also had burgers, hot dogs, and chicken—all cooked on the grill. Of course, we had a birthday cake too! But that wasn't all; Momma let both of us have a sleepover with a few friends. We all fell asleep kind of early because we were exhausted from the Caterpillar.

CHAPTER 5

# TIME TO HIDE

When Daddy was around, he took us to cool places like the park and beach. He also showed off how strong he was with his push-ups and sit-ups. He was still our superhero.

When our parents were together, they often argued, and that scared us. Momma would give me a certain look, and I would grab Kia's hand and take her upstairs. We heard lots of screaming and sometimes things breaking as we sat huddled together.

After a while, Daddy would leave the house, and we would quietly head back downstairs. I never saw my daddy hit my momma, but she often had bruises and cuts. I was too young to really understand what was happening, but I remember there were lots of tears.

CHAPTER 6

A SPECIAL DAY

Nanny Goat had a big personality. She was energetic and fun, and she said all kinds of outrageous things.

This is the best gift EVER!

In second grade, I got a $100 bill from her on my birthday.

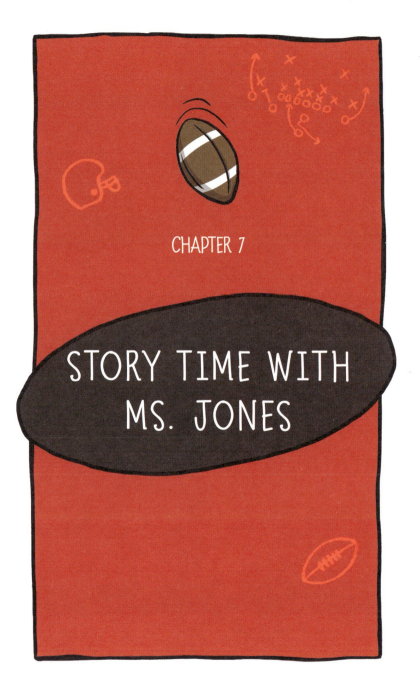

CHAPTER 7

STORY TIME WITH MS. JONES

I had some nice teachers at school, but my favorite was Ms. Jones. She welcomed each student as they entered her classroom. We all loved story time with Ms. Jones. She read the coolest books to us.

Ms. Jones used to do something else I'll never forget. She would give the student with the highest score on each test a big bag of gummy treats. I tried really hard in her class, and no one got more gummies than I did!

During story time, Ms. Jones introduced me to Harry Potter. The story was so long that she couldn't finish reading it to us in class. To buy the book was expensive, and the copies at school and in the library were almost always checked out. I eventually got a copy and finished reading that Harry Potter book. It was so good!

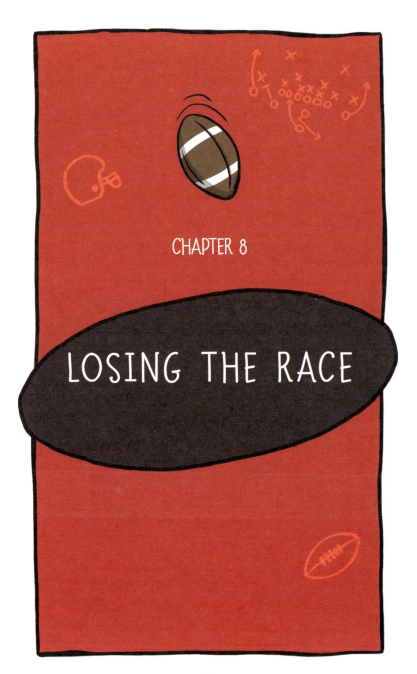

CHAPTER 8

# LOSING THE RACE

When I was six, I loved basketball and football, but I was never one of the best players in either sport.

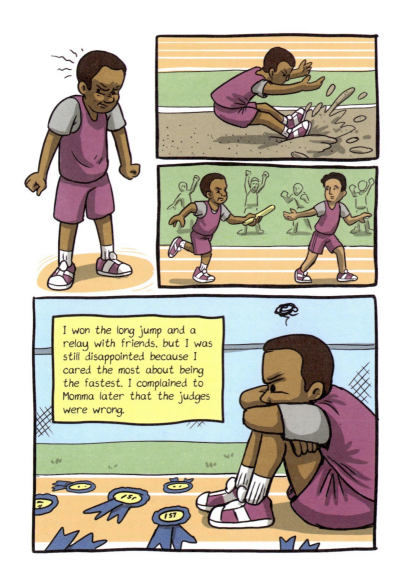

I won the long jump and a relay with friends, but I was still disappointed because I cared the most about being the fastest. I complained to Momma later that the judges were wrong.

Momma's Rule:
Some of life's best lessons
come from disappointment
and failure.

CHAPTER 9

VISITING DAD

When I was little, my daddy was arrested and put in jail for two years. Kia and I didn't know the details, but our view of him didn't change. We looked forward to visiting him in prison.

We liked talking to Daddy, hugging him, and getting snacks from the vending machines. There wasn't much else to do during our visits. Prison officials searched all visitors, and we weren't allowed to bring anything special for Daddy. Not candy or treats. Not clothes or shoes. Just some quarters for the vending machine. We didn't play games or do any activities, but somehow the two-hour visit always seemed to go too quickly.

When Daddy was at Beaumont Prison, we got to ride a ferry to visit him! Momma could only take us on Saturdays, and we couldn't spend very much time with him. The worst part was leaving him behind.

CHAPTER 10

## LIBRARY INSPIRATION

We didn't have extra money, so Momma always looked for free things to do and places to go. Nanny Goat would watch us a lot, and Kia and I liked to go to the public library with her. She didn't mind us tagging along. Sometimes she would even sneak in her pet iguana!

Nanny Goat liked to check out books on gardening and cooking. I preferred reading books and watching DVDs about important leaders and sports figures. One of my favorite leaders was Jack Johnson, nicknamed the "Galveston Giant."

Jack was famous for becoming the first African American world heavyweight champion in the early 1900s. I couldn't believe such a legend grew up near our house!

I was also mesmerized by the legendary boxer Muhammad Ali. I watched videos of him a lot. When he talked, it sounded like he was reciting poetry.

Float like a butterfly, sting like a bee. You can't hit what your eyes don't see.

The will must be stronger than the skill.

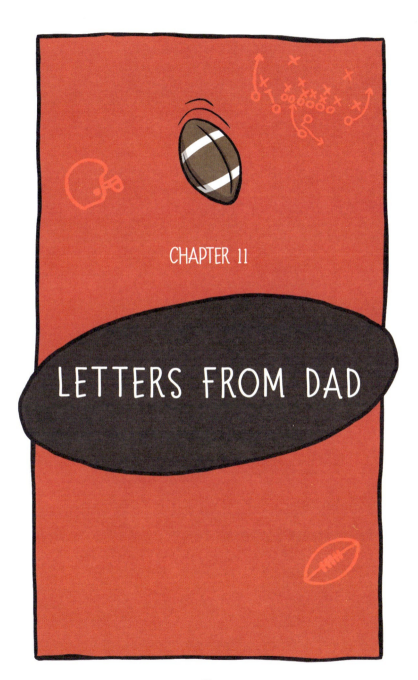

CHAPTER 11

LETTERS FROM DAD

At home, nothing excited me more than checking the mailbox. Daddy would write a letter to Kia and me each week. And even better, he would draw us pictures!

When I was learning karate, Daddy drew a picture of me doing a flying kick with Air Jordan sneakers on. I thought that was pretty cool. I loved hearing from him. It was something I looked forward to.

I never wrote to Daddy even though he always asked me to, but Kia sent him a few letters.

I know it made my dad sad not to hear from me; I just felt awkward writing to him because I didn't know what to say.

CHAPTER 12

FIRST LOVE

I loved sports, and I was competitive by nature. I even liked practice, not just the games. Playing sports gave me a chance to travel to other towns, including some in different states.

At first, I showed a lot of skill and talent in football especially as a defensive player. But I loved basketball most, probably because of Daddy's influence.

I really wanted to be the best in basketball, but several of my teammates were better. I'll never forget the time in fifth grade when I had a fastbreak, and I missed the layup—by a lot. I was so embarrassed.

My teammates didn't make me feel worse about it though. They encouraged me instead.

CHAPTER 13

WAKE-UP CALL

We lived really close to Nanny Goat. One day, I was hanging out with two boys in her neighborhood, and one of them wanted to check out the body shop across the street. There was a problem: it had a fence around it.

There were a couple of cars and trucks in the lot. One of the boys picked up a rock, then tossed another one to me and the other kid. A split second after I caught the rock, he hurled his through a car window!

I really didn't want to, but I gave in to the peer pressure.

I immediately jumped the fence and sprinted back home. The other boys followed me. We hoped no one had seen us. But about ten minutes later, the police showed up at my house. They told us there were witnesses, and they put us in the back of the police car. I was nervous and afraid.

It felt like forever, but Officer Smith finally let us out of the police car with a warning. He waited for the other boys to leave, then he pulled me aside for a special message. The officer had recognized me, and he respected—and liked—Nanny Goat. He wanted me to learn from the incident and stay out of trouble.

Officer Smith's Rule:
Don't do something just
because everyone else
is doing it.
Make better choices.

CHAPTER 14

MAKING UP FOR
LOST TIME

Kia and I were so excited when Daddy was released from prison! We had missed him very much, and now we got to see him a lot more.

He started to work as a server in a restaurant, and he saved up money to buy us gifts and take us on small adventures.

Daddy was much harder on me than he was on Kia. Maybe it was because she was younger, or maybe it was because she was a girl. I didn't know.

Once, when Daddy was eating lunch, he said he didn't want the tomato that was on his sandwich. I did.

"Oh, oh. Give it to me! Can I have it?" I asked.

Daddy snapped at me. "Don't ever beg for anything from anybody!" It was about the angriest he'd ever been with me.

Another time, Kia wanted to hang out with a friend who lived a couple blocks away. Because we didn't live in the safest neighborhood, Daddy didn't want her to walk alone. He told me to take her there.

I walked Kia to the corner near her friend's house and headed back home to continue playing video games. Kia's friend wasn't home, so she walked back to our house all by herself. Daddy was furious! He screamed at me, and then he spanked me.

Daddy's Rule:
Always look after your
sister. Always.

CHAPTER 15

# LESSONS SINK IN

Daddy had lessons for me not just for life but for sports too. In football, he constantly told me how important it was to protect the ball.

"Switch the ball away from the nearest defender," he told me.

I tried to be respectful, but I didn't always take his advice.

One time, when I was returning a kickoff in a game, I didn't switch the ball to the other side, and an opponent punched it away from me. His teammate recovered the ball. I was so embarrassed that I had turned the ball over.

Daddy watched the play, but he didn't say anything to me afterward. I'm pretty sure he was disappointed that I hadn't listened to him.

Later that night, Kia and I were woken up and rushed to Nanny Goat's house. We had no idea what was going on.

We got the worst news ever the next morning: Daddy was dead. I was shocked and had a lot of questions, but no one would tell me any details.

I felt really bad that I didn't listen to Daddy about switching the ball away from the defender. I started to think about other things he had told me, like how to shoot a basketball the right way.

I had a hard time accepting that my dad was gone. Nanny Goat told Kia and me that everyone processes death in different ways. I went back to school right away, but Kia stayed home for a few days.

One way I felt like I could honor Daddy's memory was to work on what he had been trying to teach me before he died. I committed myself to becoming a great athlete. I was going to make him proud.

Daddy's Rule:
Never settle. Work hard to get what you want in life.

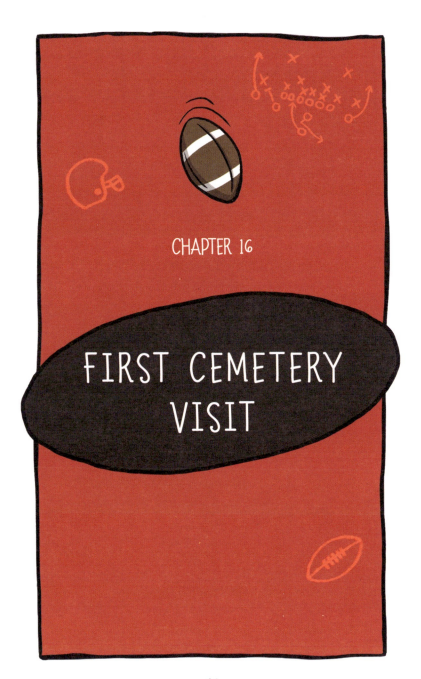

CHAPTER 16

# FIRST CEMETERY VISIT

Accepting that Daddy was no longer alive was really hard for me and Kia. It felt more real the first time we went to visit the cemetery where he was buried.

Daddy was buried in a nice cemetery almost 30 minutes away.

Kia and Momma headed back to the car, but... I wanted to stay. I really missed my dad a lot.

I wanted to do something special for Daddy, so I decided to do push-ups. I tried to do 100 in a row like Daddy would, but I couldn't do that many.

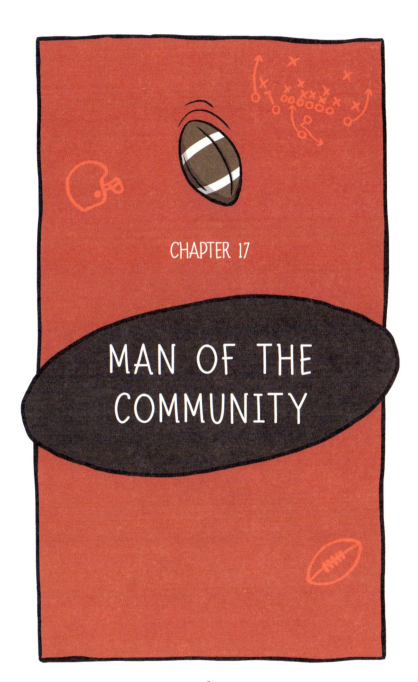

CHAPTER 17

# MAN OF THE COMMUNITY

I got more and more angry after my dad died, and I didn't know how to control my emotions. After one loss in football, I picked up a trash can and tossed it through the air. In one game when I made a bad play, I slammed my helmet onto the ground.

Sometimes when I got mad, I would start crying.

Momma was worried about me. She asked one of the community's most respected men, Terry Petteway, to mentor me. Mr. Petteway worked in the Sheriff's Department and became Galveston's first Black constable. (A constable is a licensed peace officer who performs various law enforcement duties.) This important position requires an election to office once every four years.

Petteway was also a very respected coach, but I didn't like him after our first practice. Momma didn't care. She told me, "You're going back!"

Coach Petteway was patient with me. He helped me to calm down, stay focused, and ignore what opponents said and did instead of starting a fight.

Coach Petteway's Rule: You can't get violent just because someone says something you don't like. At the end of the day, it's only words.

Coach Petteway looked after me a lot. I didn't mind because his son Terran played football and basketball with me, and he was a very good athlete. We competed hard in practice, and we made each other better. When I did well, Coach Petteway was always there to celebrate with me.

When he was in the Sheriff's department, Coach Petteway worked in the jail. He was saddened by the high number of Black men who wound up there, including some of his childhood friends and classmates. The main reason he decided to become a coach was that he thought it would help make a difference in the lives of young Black men.

"Coaching gives me an opportunity to invest in the community," Coach Petteway said. "I become a second dad to a lot of guys."

Coach Petteway could relate to many of his players who didn't have it easy at home. He grew up in public housing which are homes made available by the government to low-income families.

Coach Petteway loved sports, and he was very competitive. He encouraged his players to be their best physically, academically, and mentally. He was just as proud of those who went on to play football in college as he was of the kids who focused on getting their degrees.

CHAPTER 18

# REVENGE RACE

CHAPTER 19

# THE BEST SHE COULD

Momma had my brother Donovan—who everyone called Booja—about eight years after I was born. I don't know how Momma did it with three kids, but we always had great Christmas and birthday gifts. Kia, Booja, and I would get the latest toys and clothes.

We weren't rich. Sometimes our gas and electricity would be shut off, and Momma would stress out about all the different bills. At times there wasn't enough money in her bank account to cover the checks she had written.

There was a reason Momma wanted us to have stuff: when she was in middle school, she showed up for the first day of school in shoes that had holes in them. Other kids made fun of her, and she felt humiliated. She never wanted her kids to experience the same thing.

Momma encouraged us to look good which is why she worked so hard to buy us cool clothes. She thought a person's appearance was important.

**Momma's Rule:**
**Always look nice. What if the President were coming over?**

Things were rough, but Momma worked really hard and never gave up. She graduated from high school and earned an associate degree in college. When she became a nurse, she worked the late shift. This meant she was at the hospital at night while we were home sleeping, and she slept during the day.

One day, I heard about a basketball shooting contest, and I thought about waking her up, so she could drive me to the gym. Instead, I rode a scooter she had bought me for Christmas. There were a bunch of kids in the competition, but I won, and I rode home on my scooter with the trophy!

CHAPTER 20

PRO PERSPECTIVE

I admired the "Galveston Giant" boxing champion, Jack Johnson, but there was another hometown athlete who I could actually watch on TV. His name was Casey Hampton, and he had starred at Ball High School in Galveston and then at the University of Texas where he was a two-time All-American.

Casey played 12 seasons in the NFL for the Pittsburgh Steelers and was a five-time Pro Bowl selection. He hosted a football camp for kids in my area, and he would pull up in a fancy SUV with shiny rims.

I started going to Casey's camp when I was nine years old. Being one of the younger players, I wasn't as fast as most of the older kids. I didn't catch any of the passes thrown my way. That taught me not to be overconfident. Casey raced us and shared positive messages with us.

He pulled me aside one time because he noticed

I was always going as fast as I could, trying to keep up. He assured me, "The game will slow down for you." Casey's point was that the more I practiced and played, the more comfortable I would be with everything: running routes, catching the ball, making opponents miss, and more.

I sure hoped Casey was right!

Casey Hampton's Rule:
Stay humble, be coachable, and have fun. You'll get everything you want from the game.

Casey accomplished a lot individually. He was a two-time Super Bowl champion with the Steelers, and Galveston threw him a parade after each victory. He rode in a big truck or on a float, tossing out beads and candy.

No matter how much money he made or how much he accomplished, Casey always represented his hometown well and paid it forward with kids like me. I wanted to do that too.

CHAPTER 21

ALWAYS THERE

Sometimes you consider people family even though they aren't actually related to you. Aunt Josephine was one of those people. She connected right away with my mom in sixth grade. The day Momma showed up to school with holes in her shoes, Aunt Josephine's mom took her to the store and bought her new ones.

Josephine had five older siblings, but she was the youngest by many years. So, she and Momma became really close, like sisters.

Momma was young when she had me and Kia, and she lost a lot of her friends—but not Aunt Josephine. When Momma needed help, Aunt Josephine always did her best to provide it.

Aunt Josephine was also my godmother. That means my momma officially asked Josephine to help raise me. Many people consider being a godparent a very special honor. Aunt Josephine took it seriously.

Sometimes she spoiled me with treats and gifts. Other times she stepped up to pay for things my family couldn't afford, like when I needed lessons to get my driver's license.

Even more important, Aunt Josephine came to most of my games and always said nice, encouraging things to me, while others doubted my dreams of becoming a professional athlete.

Aunt Josephine told me to keep trying my best in school and sports and to avoid the kids who often got into trouble.

Aunt Josephine's Rule:
Never give up on your dream.

CHAPTER 22

SLEEP CHALLENGES

When I was awake, I was active. My body felt tired when it was bedtime, but I struggled most nights to fall asleep. The longer the night got, the more anxious I became.

When I finally dozed off, I slept hard.

CHAPTER 23

MOTIVATING MIKE

I was a pretty motivated kid especially when it came to sports. I wasn't afraid to work hard in practices and games, and I didn't need much to persuade me. Sometimes, though, Momma would reward me after a big game with a double cheeseburger and spicy chicken sandwich from my favorite fast-food restaurant!

As he got to know me better, Coach Petteway figured out just how competitive I was. He sometimes doubted my athletic ability, like whether or not I could make a shot or guard somebody. This made me want to prove to him I could rise to the occasion and help our team.

We didn't have the biggest players on our basketball team. Coach Petteway would look at our opponents and say, "Oh man. Look at them big boys!"

I was never afraid of bigger kids. As I improved in basketball and football, Coach Petteway reminded me not to get comfortable. He said the biggest dreams were the hardest to make a reality.

Coach Petteway's Rule:
You have to work for
what you want.

Coach Petteway really appreciated my commitment. I never missed a practice, and I didn't show up late. If we were supposed to arrive at 6 p.m., I'd get there by 5:40 p.m. Coach told me that I was a "gym rat." I liked that.

CHAPTER 24

# IRON SHARPENS IRON

I had some great teammates and friends growing up, like Dietrich and Greg. But the person who pushed me the most was Terran. We both really wanted to go far in sports and weren't afraid to work toward that goal.

We would battle so hard in practices, Coach would sometimes have to call for a break, so we could cool down.

In football, Terran was the quarterback and middle linebacker, and I was a tight end and defensive end. When the game was on the line, Coach would draw up a play for me to get the ball.

As competitive as Terran and I were, we were also each other's biggest fans on the field or court. He would celebrate my success, and I would celebrate his.

The most important thing was that we helped our team. Coach Petteway pushed us to be tough, to work hard, and to always have each other's backs. Terran and I made sure our teammates did those things too.

Be tough, work hard, and have each other's back.
—Coach Petteway

There were a lot of great basketball players and teams in Texas. We won some of our tournaments, and that always felt good!

CHAPTER 25

NO "I" IN TEAM

I was doing better at basketball, but I still made a lot of mistakes. We were playing in the Great American Shootout—a big basketball tournament—and I had hurt my knee. Coach didn't think I was moving very well, so he subbed me out of the game. I was really mad because I wanted to keep playing.

I let my frustration get the best of me. When one of my teammate's shots got blocked, I yelled from our bench, "Good block!" When our opponents scored, I cheered.

Upset and disappointed, Coach Petteway glared at me and said, "You're off the team!" He told me to grab my stuff and leave.

I left the bench, but I figured Coach was joking about me not playing on his team anymore. I wasn't laughing when he didn't pick me up for the next tournament.

"He left me," I told Coach Petteway's oldest son, Terrell. "I can't believe it."

Terrell told me not to get too discouraged and to look for the lesson Coach might be trying to teach me.

The next chance I got, I apologized to him for my behavior at the Great American Shootout.

Coach Petteway's Rule:
There are consequences for
your actions. Learn from
your mistakes.

CHAPTER 26

ROUGH STRETCH

In high school, I really didn't want to listen to anybody...including Momma. I had a bad attitude and made a point of ignoring her. I just wanted to play video games and hang out with my friends. It got so bad that Momma kicked me out of the house! This

happened a few times, and it was never for more than a few days, but, I wasn't easy to live with then.

I was struggling with a lot during this time.

I failed my biology class because I didn't study enough. I was so distracted by other things, and Advanced Placement Biology was really, really hard.

As I was walking between the school and the football field once, I got jumped by some gang members. I was by myself near the concession stand, and I don't know why they did it. The three of them beat me up, and I had a big cut close to my eye.

Another time, I was involved in a fight with a rival sports team. As discipline, I had to serve a three-week, in-school suspension. I couldn't talk to any other students, and I had no teachers helping me with my classwork.

I did something even more awful during this stage of my life. Momma still worked at night, and she often expected me to watch my little brother while she slept.

Once I was hanging out on the porch with a friend, not watching Booja closely enough. A few minutes passed, and I heard car tires screech, then saw my little brother flying through the air. He had gotten hit by a car!

When I ran over to him, I thought he was dead. Thankfully, he was breathing, and then he started moving his arms and legs. I began to cry; I was so grateful he was alive.

I swore I would start being more responsible.

CHAPTER 27

HURRICANE IKE

Residents of Galveston were used to hurricanes and storms. Texas is the second-most state affected by hurricanes, with only Florida in front of it. But many people weren't ready for the severity of Hurricane Ike in 2008.

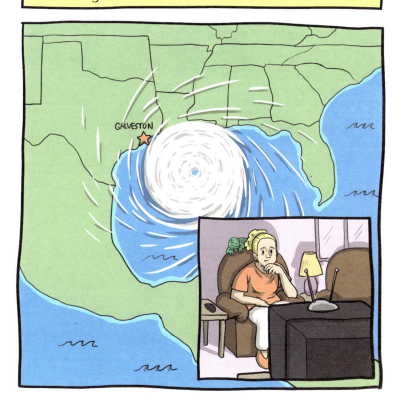

Hurricane Ike was a massive storm with winds gusting up to 143 miles per hour. It caused $38 billion in damage.

What was normally a 52-minute drive from Galveston to Houston took us 11 hours.

Most residents in Galveston fled their homes, but Nanny Goat refused to leave. She stayed in her house with her pets.

Meanwhile, my family bounced around from hotel to hotel, in different cities, for months because our home was so badly damaged. I even had to sleep on the floor sometimes.

Momma's Rule:
You have to be able to adjust and adapt. The most important thing is that we're all healthy and safe.

Our family had to wait for several months, but our house was finally repaired, and it looked better than ever!

CHAPTER 28

HOOPS DREAM

There was no doubt that I was a good football player, and I was confident about my performance during tryouts in my freshman year at Ball High School. The football team relied on a heavy run offense and didn't value my strengths as a receiver.

When the rosters were posted, I discovered that
the coaches hadn't put me on the A team with my
friends. Seeing my name on the B team list made
me really mad, so I decided not to play football and
turned my focus to basketball instead.

Being fully dedicated to basketball started to pay off. Our AAU team was doing really well, and people were noticing me. Coaches from big programs like Texas Tech, the University of Virginia, and Wichita State University started talking to me about playing in their programs. I was feeling good about my future in basketball.

CHAPTER 29

HELPING OTHERS

Momma never had a lot of money, but that didn't stop her from being very generous. Not many people helped her with me and Kia, so she decided to be different and help others.

Momma let us have sleepovers, and we often invited friends over for dinner and snacks. If any of my friends needed a place to stay, Momma always had room for them.

When my friend Dietrich told me his family had  to move due to financial hardship, I asked Momma if he could live with us. Dietrich didn't want to switch school districts.

Momma let him stay for our junior and senior years in high school! He slept in my bedroom, and we shared everything. I had nice clothes but not a lot of them. Sometimes I would wear an outfit, then wash it, and Dietrich would wear it another day.

Letting my friend stay with us so he could finish high school was just one great example of Momma's generosity.

Dietrich and I were best friends. Others thought we'd get sick of each other since we were together *all the time*. We had lots of classes together, and we were on the same teams. But we also chose to spend our free time together, playing video games and going to the movies—especially if a new Harry Potter movie was out! We liked a lot of the same things, and we enjoyed each other's company.

CHAPTER 30

RUNNING TRACK

My friends and I were looking forward to a relaxing spring as we inched closer to graduation. But Coach Petteway had a different idea...

You're all going to run track. You're not just sitting around.

We started to get the hang of relay running, and we regularly won our races.

But we got nervous as we prepared to face far more experienced teams at the district meet.

We were disappointed when we lost, but our family and friends were proud of us especially since most of us had never run track before.

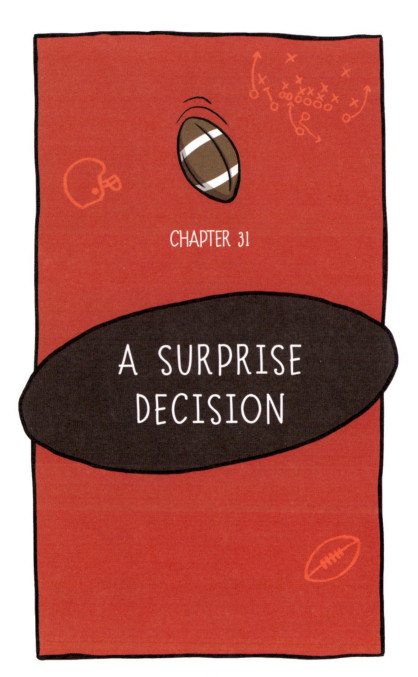

CHAPTER 31

A SURPRISE DECISION

My friends who played football asked me every season to try out for the school team. I finally gave in my senior year. I wanted the experience. Basketball remained my favorite sport, but I wanted to see if I still had my football skills. And I wanted to spend as much time with my friends as possible.

Our team struggled, but that didn't stop me from playing hard and with passion. Some college football coaches were impressed with my talent. They were usually at our games to evaluate players on the opposing team's roster. But they couldn't ignore me on the field—neither could the defenders. One time I stiff-armed an opponent so hard, he dropped to the ground.

Everyone expected me to play college basketball, but I went on an unofficial visit to Texas A&M's football program, and that really made me think. I watched the Aggies practice before a big game, and I marveled at their stadium, Kyle Field, which holds more than 100,000 fans!

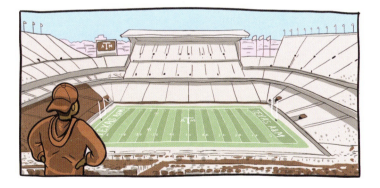

I had multiple basketball scholarship offers, and that was my favorite sport growing up, but I also loved football. When it came time to decide between the two, I went with my heart and signed on to play football at Texas A&M.

It was a difficult decision, but I felt it was the right one. I knew I had the support of many people, including Coach Petteway, Aunt Josephine, Nanny Goat, Kia, Booja, and, most importantly, Momma. They had stood by me when times were rough, and I knew they would continue to encourage me to reach for my dreams.

# EPILOGUE

During his senior year at Ball High, Mike Evans caught 25 passes for 648 yards and seven touchdowns. He also added two interceptions on defense. For the Tors basketball team, Mike averaged 18.3 points, 8.4 rebounds, and 5.2 assists per game.

Known more as a basketball player, Mike drew interest from notable programs such as Houston, Virginia, and Colorado State. In football, he was a three-star recruit, according to Scout.com, ranking as the 94th best prospect at his position. Football programs such as Tulane tracked Mike, but the football and basketball coaches at Texas A&M both liked him as a student-athlete.

Like many athletes transitioning from high school to college, Mike redshirted his freshman year at A&M, which means he did not play in games. He focused on his academics, and increased his strength, stamina, and understanding of the team's playbook.

In his first year playing, Mike dominated, serving as the top target for quarterback Johnny Manziel, who would become the first freshman to ever win the Heisman Trophy, college football's top honor.

Mike started all 13 games and led the Aggies with 82 catches for 1,105 yards and five touchdowns. In his second season, he was named a first-team All-American, and he once again led the Aggies in catches (69) and receiving yards (1,394) and scored 12 touchdowns.

A finalist for the Biletnikoff Award given annually to the nation's top receiver, Mike shined against his opponents. He caught 11 passes for 287 yards and four touchdowns against Auburn, and seven passes for 279 yards and one touchdown against Alabama.

In January 2014, Mike announced that he would make himself available for the 2014 NFL Draft, and he was selected seventh overall by the Tampa Bay Buccaneers. He immediately asserted himself, utilizing his rare combination of size (6 feet 5 inches, 231 pounds) and athleticism (4.53 seconds in the 40-yard dash and a 37-inch vertical leap).

Mike has been selected to the Pro Bowl four times,

and he was an All-Pro in 2016. He is the only player in NFL history to have started his career with eight consecutive seasons with at least 1,000 receiving yards!

Mike has earned the respect of his teammates, fans, and coaches with his work ethic and commitment to the team.

"He's a workaholic, and he's a very selfless guy," head coach Bruce Arians told radio station WDAE in December 2020. "He's the most unselfish star receiver that I've ever been around."

Tom Brady, arguably the greatest player in NFL history, was also very

complimentary of Mike, calling him one of the great all-time receivers and a future Hall of Fame player.

The 2020 NFL season was a special one, as the Bucs capped it with a 31-9 Super Bowl victory over the Kansas City Chiefs.

In March 2021, Mike fulfilled a childhood dream when his hometown of Galveston hosted a parade in his honor, similar to the one he was inspired by for Casey Hampton.

Wanting to do something extra special, Mike signed posters and slipped $20 or $100 bills into each one for local kids who looked up to him.

Galveston Mayor Craig Brown declared March 26 to be "Mike Evans Day" in the city.

"It's an unbelievable feeling coming from a city

that I love," Evans told The
Daily News of Galveston
County—the oldest
newspaper in Texas. "It's
surreal. I'm really looking
forward to seeing all the
faces that I saw as a

kid. There's still a lot of people I know. It's
a great city, and I'm truly honored."

In September 2022, Mike was inducted into Texas
A&M's Athletics Hall of Fame, alongside former
teammates Johnny Manziel and Luke Joeckel.

Mike and his wife, Ashli, have always prioritized
helping others. They created the Mike Evans Family
Foundation in December 2017. The foundation focuses

on empowering youth, encouraging education, and taking a stand against domestic violence.

After his father died when he was nine, Mike confronted many challenges and was encouraged and supported by family members and community leaders including Coach Terry Petteway.

Mike knows the impact that caring adults can have on young people, and he wants to help and inspire as many kids as he can. Like Casey Hampton, Mike hosts a free football camp in Galveston.

Just before his parade in 2021, his foundation donated $50,000 to the United Way of Galveston to help families affected by storms.

Mike is the father of four children: Mackenzie, Ariah, Amari, and Aliyah.

Mike Evans' Life Rule:
Don't run from adversity.
It shows you who you really
are and helps you to become a
better person. The challenges
early in my life molded me
into the man I am today.

# ACKNOWLEDGMENTS
## FROM MIKE EVANS

I want to thank my mom for being the best mom ever and for giving us everything we needed to succeed. She had it tough, but she made it work for us. Without her, I would not be where I am or who I am today.

Thanks to my wonderful wife, Ashli, for being my best friend and amazing mother to our children.

Mackenzie, Ariah, Amari, and Aliyah, you are the best kids a parent could ask for. Thanks for being so cool!

Thank you to everyone who was interviewed for this book, and all of my friends and family, including my sister, Mikia, and brothers, Donovan and Malik.

I would also like to express my gratitude to the city of Galveston, Texas A&M University, the Tampa Bay Buccaneers, and all of my coaches and teammates. Thank you all for making me who I am and giving me memories that I will cherish forever.

# FROM SEAN JENSEN

These last few years have been hard, but I thank God for his constant love and grace.

I am thankful, as always, to my incredible wife, Erica, for her love and support, and for the encouragement and inspiration of my children, Elijah and Zarah.

I also want to thank agent Deryk Gilmore of Day 1 Sports and Entertainment for making the initial introduction to Mike Evans, and Julie Magrane of Priority Sports for helping me throughout this process.

Thanks to the amazing illustrator, Daniel Hawkins, and my brilliant team at BroadStreet Publishing—Michelle, Chris, and Carlton.

I would be remiss if I didn't thank Mike and his family for their patience and trust in allowing me to tell their stories.

# ABOUT THE AUTHOR

SEAN JENSEN was born in South Korea. He was adopted and grew up in California, Massachusetts, and Virginia, mostly on or near military bases. Given his unique background, Sean has always been drawn to storytelling, a skill he developed at Northwestern University and crafted as a sportswriter—almost exclusively covering the NFL.

During his career, Sean has fostered strong relationships throughout professional sports. He is an inspirational speaker who hosts a weekly podcast called "Winning Is Not Everything." The podcast aims to bring sanity back to youth sports through conversations with high-character athletes, coaches, and parents.

Sean lives in Minneapolis with his wife, two kids, and a dog.